What's Under Your Hat?
And Other Mysteries And Riddles

Selected by Myra Barrs and Sue Ellis

Illustrated by Rachel Merriman

WALKER BOOKS
AND SUBSIDIARIES
LONDON · BOSTON · SYDNEY · AUCKLAND

THE DOOR

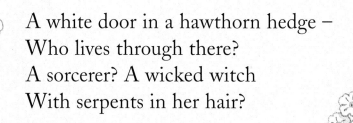

A white door in a hawthorn hedge –
Who lives through there?
A sorcerer? A wicked witch
With serpents in her hair?

A king enchanted into stone?
A lost princess?
A servant girl who works all night
Spinning a cobweb dress?

A queen with slippers made of ice?
I'd love to see.
A white door in a hawthorn hedge –
I wish I had a key.

Richard Edwards

What Is Pink?

What is pink? a rose is pink
By the fountain's brink.

What is red? a poppy's red
In its barley bed.

What is blue? the sky is blue
Where the clouds float thro'.

What is white? a swan is white
Sailing in the light.

What is yellow? pears are yellow,
Rich and ripe and mellow.

Christina Rossetti

TAM SNOW

(to Kaye Webb)

Who in the bleak wood
Barefoot, ice-fingered,
Runs to and fro?
            Tam Snow.

Who, soft as a ghost,
Falls on our house to strike
Blow after blow?
            Tam Snow.

Who with a touch of the hand
Stills the world's sound
In its flow?
            Tam Snow.

Who holds to our side,
Though as friend or as foe
We never may know?

Tam Snow.

Who hides in the hedge
After thaw, waits for more
Of his kind to show?

Tam Snow.

Who is the guest
First we welcome, then
Long to see go?

Tam Snow.

Charles Causley

WHAT HAS HAPPENED TO LULU?

What has happened to Lulu, mother?
  What has happened to Lu?
There's nothing in her bed but an old rag-doll
  And by its side a shoe.

 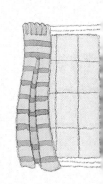

Why is her window wide, mother,
  The curtain flapping free,
And only a circle on the dusty shelf
  Where her money-box used to be?

Why do you turn your head, mother,
  And why do the tear-drops fall?
And why do you crumple that note on the fire
  And say it is nothing at all?

I woke to voices late last night,
    I heard an engine roar.
Why do you tell me the things I heard
    Were a dream and nothing more?

I heard somebody cry, mother,
    In anger or in pain,
But now I ask you why, mother,
    You say it was a gust of rain.

Why do you wander about as though
    You don't know what to do?
What has happened to Lulu, mother?
    What has happened to Lu?

Charles Causley

Where Does Laughter Begin?

Does it start in your head
and spread to your toe?

Does it start in your cheeks
and grow downwards so
till your knees feel weak?

Does it start with a tickle
in your tummy so
till you want to jump right out

of all your skin?
Or does laughter simply begin

with your mouth?

John Agard

Riddle me!
Riddle me!
What is that:
Over your head
And under your hat?

Traditional

GUESS ME

Dear Reader,
      Guess me, I'm a riddle,
What's now my end
      was once my middle.
I don't wear fur
      or hair or wings,
My body's dressed
      in shiny rings.
I love the heap,
      I love the dark,
With twisting towers
      I leave my mark,
And move my pointed,
      questing nose
Not to, but underneath
      the rose.

Now ask me what
        I like to eat:
Old leaves and things,
        I won't touch meat,
And neither,
        if I had my wish,
Would Mr Mole
        or Mrs Fish.
Fantastic tunnels,
        close and curled,
Allow me through
        the underworld,
I wiggle, turn
        and sometimes squirm,
Yes, now you've guessed,
        Your best friend,

Richard Edwards

Riddle my this, riddle my that –
  guess my riddle or perhaps not.
Boy is sent for something;
  something comes back before boy – why?

    – Boy climbs tree, picks
    coconut and drops it.

Riddle my this, riddle my that –
  guess my riddle or perhaps not.
Eyes ablaze looking up,
Four-Legs crouch near Four-Legs –
what is it?

    – Dog by dinner table
    begging.

James Berry

There was a little green house,

And in the little green house,

There was a little brown house,

And in the little brown house,

There was a little yellow house,

And in the little yellow house,

There was a little white house,

And in the little white house,

There was a little heart.

Traditional

GUESS

My first is in rattle but not in creak

My second's in creak but not in squeak

My third is in squeak and also in squeal

My fourth is in whistle and also in shrill

My fifth is in clanking and clanging and iron

My whole is the monster who roars on the line.

Berlie Doherty

RIDDLE

Although it runs
It cannot walk:
Although it turns
It can't go back.
Although it falls
It cannot break:
Although it calls
It cannot speak.

William Soutar

RIVER

boat-carrier

bank-lapper

home-provider

tree-reflector

leaf-catcher

field-wanderer

stone-smoother

fast-mover

gentle-stroller

sun-sparkler

sea-seeker

June Crebbin

CITY RIVER

wall-slapper

factory-passer

rubbish-receiver

backstreet-winder

bridge-nudger

steps-licker

park-wanderer

summer-shiner

ducks-supporter

choppy-water

crowd-delighter

onward-traveller

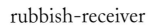

June Crebbin

CLEARING OUT

On Monday
There were skeletons under my bed,
I tickled them out with a feather duster
And locked them in the wardrobe.

On Tuesday
There were snakes under my bed,
I wrestled them into granny knots
And locked them in the wardrobe.

On Wednesday
There were scorpions under my bed,
I lured them out with a trail of honey
And locked them in the wardrobe.

On Thursday
There were ghosts under my bed,
I bundled them up like newspapers
And locked them in the wardrobe.

On Friday
We moved to our new house,
Packing everything into the lorry,
Leaving only the wardrobe behind.

Richard Edwards

PLUM

Don't be so glum,
plum.

Don't feel beaten.

You were made
to be eaten.

But don't you know
that deep within,
beneath your juicy flesh
and flimsy skin,

you bear a mystery,
you hold a key,

you have the making of
a whole new tree.

Tony Mitton

TIMELESS

There is no clock in the forest
but a dandelion to blow,
an owl that hunts
when the light has gone,
a mouse that sleeps
till night has come,
lost in the moss below.

There is no clock in the forest,
only the cuckoo's song
and the thin white
of the early dawn,
the pale damp-bright
of a waking June,
the bluebell light
of a day half-born
when the stars have gone.

There is no clock in the forest.

Judith Nicholls

IN MY GARDEN

In my garden
Grows a tree
Dances day
And night for me,
Four in a bar
Or sometimes three
To music secret
As can be.

Nightly to
Its hidden tune
I watch it move
Against the moon,
Dancing to
A silent sound,
One foot planted
In the ground.

Dancing tree,
When may I hear
Day or night
Your music clear?
What the note
And what the song
That you sing
The seasons long?

It is written,
Said the tree,
On the pages
Of the sea;
It is there
At every hand
On the pages
Of the land;

Whether waking
Or in dream:
Voice of meadow-grass
And stream,
And out of
The ringing air
Voice of sun
And moon and star.

It is there
For all to know
As tides shall turn
And wildflowers grow;
There for you
And there for me,
Said the glancing
Dancing tree.

Charles Causley

THE HORSEMAN

I heard a horseman
  Ride over the hill;
The moon shone clear,
  The night was still;
His helm was silver,
  And pale was he;
And the horse he rode
  Was of ivory.

Walter de la Mare

THE VOICE

As I sat in the gloaming
I heard a voice say,
Weep no more, sigh no more;
Come, come away!

It was dusk at the window;
From down in the street
No rumble of carts came,
No passing of feet.

I sat very still,
Too frightened to play;
And again the voice called me,
Little boy, come away!

Dark, darker it grew;
Stars came out, and the moon
Shone clear through the glass
The carpet upon.

I listened and listened;
But no more would it say –
The voice that had called me,
Come, come away!

Walter de la Mare

OTHER READ ME BOOKS

Read Me Beginners are simple rhymes and stories ideal for children learning to read.

Caveman Dave
Nick Sharratt

Monday Run-day
Nick Sharratt

Mrs Pirate
Nick Sharratt

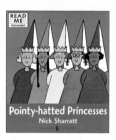

Pointy-hatted Princesses
Nick Sharratt

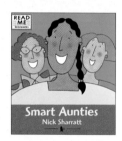

Smart Aunties
Nick Sharratt

The Green Queen
Nick Sharratt

Read Me Story Plays are dramatized versions of favourite stories, written for four or more voices to share.

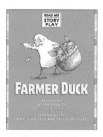

FARMER DUCK
RE-PLAYED BY
VIVIAN FRENCH
FROM THE BOOK BY
MARTIN WADDELL AND HELEN OXENBURY

THIS IS THE BEAR
RE-PLAYED BY
VIVIAN FRENCH
FROM THE BOOK BY
SARAH HAYES AND HELEN CRAIG

WE'RE GOING ON A BEAR HUNT
RE-PLAYED BY
VIVIAN FRENCH
FROM THE BOOK BY
MICHAEL ROSEN AND HELEN OXENBURY

Little Rabbit Foo Foo
RE-PLAYED BY
VIVIAN FRENCH
FROM THE BOOK BY
MICHAEL ROSEN AND ARTHUR ROBINS

The Three Little Pigs
WRITTEN BY
VIVIAN FRENCH
ILLUSTRATED BY
LIZ PICHON

Jack and the Beanstalk
WRITTEN BY
VIVIAN FRENCH
ILLUSTRATED BY
HARRY HORSE

The Three Billy-Goats Gruff
WRITTEN BY
VIVIAN FRENCH
ILLUSTRATED BY
ARTHUR ROBINS

The Gingerbread Boy
WRITTEN BY
VIVIAN FRENCH
ILLUSTRATED BY
JOHN PRATER